COMBAT AIRCRAFT

B-1b
Bomber

LINDSAY PEACOCK

OSPREY PUBLISHING LONDON

Published in 1987 by
Osprey Publishing Ltd
Member Company of the George Philip Group
12–14 Long Acre, London WC2E 9LP

British Library Cataloguing in Publication Data

Peacock, Lindsay T.
    Rockwell B-1.–(Osprey combat aircraft)
    1. B-1 bomber
    I. Title
    623.74'63   UG1242.B6

ISBN 0-85045-750-5

Typeset by Flair plan Photo-typesetting Ltd.
Printed by Proost International Book Production,
Turnhout, Belgium.

Designed by Little Oak Studios
Colour artworks: Terry Hadler and Mike Keep
Cutaway drawing: © Pilot Press Ltd.
Photographs: The publishers thank Rockwell
International and the United States Department of
Defense for supplying the photographs reproduced in this
book.

The Author
LINDSAY PEACOCK is an aviation journalist and
photographer who has written extensively on military
aircraft subjects for books and magazines, especially in
areas of specific interest to aircraft modellers. He has
travelled widely in pursuit of his profession and hobbies,
and spent much time at military aircraft establishments
observing his subjects at close quarters. His other books in
this series are *F/A-18 Hornet*, *F-14 Tomcat*, *B-52 Stratofortress*
and the forthcoming *AH-1 HueyCobra*.

Contents

1

Background and Development

THERE can be few modern warplanes that have experienced quite such a protracted development period as the Rockwell B-1 strategic bomber nor have there been many which have suffered the indignity of cancellation, only to reappear in a slightly different guise. Now in the process of joining the Strategic Air Command (SAC) inventory as the B-1B, it has yet to acquire a name but in view of its past history there would appear to be only one suitable candidate, namely "Phoenix", this being particularly apposite in that it relates to a mythical flying creature which consumes itself by fire every 500 years or so, only to reappear from its own ashes.

In truth, of course, the B-1's career hasn't been quite so dramatic as that of the mythical flying creature, it being more a victim of other considerations than of a desire to self-destruct. For instance, cancellation in the summer of 1977 was partly a political decision (the then-President of the USA, Jimmy Carter, was hopeful of a satisfactory outcome in continuing arms reduction negotiations with the USSR), partly a cost-saving measure (unit cost per B-1A was then expected to top the $100 million mark) and partly due to the advent of new weapons (notably the much cheaper air-launched cruise missile (ALCM) which seemed to offer an excellent chance of boosting deterrent capability at relatively modest financial outlay).

As we now know, the arms reduction talks failed to lead to any meaningful concessions, the new administration headed by President Ronald Reagan seemed hell-bent on pursuing a "money no object" philosophy in the defence context and, finally and perhaps most ironic of all, the developed B-1B was being viewed as an ideal vehicle to carry the weapon which so nearly caused its demise, namely the Boeing AGM-86 ALCM. In many ways, though, the B-1B is perceived as a stop-gap solution, being intended to fulfil the penetration task until such time as the much

Below: Fabricated largely from wood, this 45,000lb mock-up played an important part in the building of the first flyable B-1A by serving as a guide for both engineering and manufacturing processes performed by Rockwell and key sub-contractors.

talked about but little publicized Northrop B-2 Advanced Technology Bomber (ATB) becomes available in the mid-1990s.

However, in the light of recent attempts to develop new bomber aircraft in the USA, it is by no means inconceivable that the B-2 could fall foul of what might best be described as the "we've been through this movie before" syndrome, itself a possible candidate for cancellation on the grounds of cost, political considerations or the advent of new weapons. In view of that and the fact that the manned bomber portion of SAC's deterrent capability has in recent years been predicated pretty much on a policy of making the best of what is available, the B-1B may well now be embarking on a very long career.

Fortunately, SAC has acquired considerable expertise in what could be called the "make do and mend" strategy as the history of the Boeing B-52 Stratofortress will quickly confirm. Whether the command faces with enthusiasm the prospect of applying the same philosophy to the B-1B—a type which is in many ways a compromise, albeit a good one—is open to debate, but there is always the distinct possibility that it may not have much choice. Time will tell.

After years of having more or less its own way with regard to the procurement of bomber aircraft, SAC's good fortune in this direction came to an abrupt end on 26 October 1962 when the last examples of the B-52 and the B-58 Hustler were handed over. With the exception of 76 General Dynamics FB-111As—a

type which, while admirable in many ways, was hardly the custom-built machine that SAC would have chosen had it been able to—no more new bomber aircraft were to join the command for more than 20 years.

Of course, nobody knew that at the time and, indeed, the Air Force was even then engaged in exploratory studies intended to result in a new bomber for service with SAC. In the event, it was to take a quarter of a century before any hardware actually reached the command, this interval being perhaps most memorable for the remarkable number of acronyms which came and went while the service endeavoured to define precisely what it wanted. To those with a penchant for "alphabet soup", the new bomber provided a golden opportunity and during the next 15 years or so, acronym succeeded acronym as the project took on more tangible shape: SLAB, AMP, LAMP, AMSA, NTP, CMCA, MRB and LRCA represented some of the more significant stages in development.

"Project Forecast"

Initial studies were accomplished under a generic classification as the Subsonic Low Altitude Bomber

(SLAB). This work got under way in 1961 and was followed in 1962 by "Project Forecast" which was, in broad terms, a seven-year evaluation of the direction that strategic deterrence should take. In consequence, it encompassed not only manned bomber resources but also land- and sea-based ballistic missiles, and one of the key conclusions was that there was still a place for the manned bomber which had the priceless advantage of being able to be recalled. In addition, of course, it was far more flexible for it could also perform conventional bombing missions.

"Project Forecast" was, however, merely an incidental factor in the saga of what ultimately evolved into the B-1 although it did at least have the merit of confirming that there was indeed still a requirement for bombers. In the meantime, 1963 heralded a quite dramatic proliferation of acronyms, no fewer than four bomber-related studies getting under way. Two were undertaken by the USAF itself, these being known as the Extended Range Strategic Aircraft (ERSA) and Low Altitude Manned Penetrator (LAMP), while government money funded two more

broad-based studies accomplished by industry and known as the Advanced Manned Penetrator (AMP) and Advanced Manned Penetrating Strategic System (AMPSS).

Two years later, the best features of these disparate studies provided a basis for the Advanced Manned Strategic Aircraft (AMSA), this four-year effort being financed by the Air Force and undertaken by Boeing, General Dynamics and North American Rockwell. At that time, the basic task of any forthcoming AMSA type was perceived as being the deterrence of nuclear war, an objective which, in theory, should have been accomplished by virtue of its very existence.

In reality, though, it was perhaps rather more complex than that, AMSA being expected to possess the ability to survive a nuclear attack before penetrating existing or projected enemy defences to deliver a

Below: Once airborne, little time was wasted in extending the B-1A's flight envelope, and the use of in-flight refuelling from KC-135As permitted long sorties to be flown, thus maximising the amount of data generated whilst aloft.

retaliatory strike with either stand-off or gravity weapons. This essentially meant that any new bomber should be a significant improvement over the B-52 in terms of survivability, penetration capability and payload/range characteristics.

Contract awarded

While these studies were under way, the Defense Systems Acquisition Review Council (DSARC) began contract definition work on what would eventually become the B-1 in July 1967, and this in turn led to the USAF issuing a request for proposals (RFP) from industry in December 1969, all three companies involved in the AMSA project responding in early 1970. After evaluating the various submissions, USAF adjudged Rockwell's contender to be the most suitable and this was duly awarded a full-scale development contract in early June 1970. General Electric was chosen to produce the engines which would power the new bomber, now officially known as the B-1. The initial contract covered the manufacture of five flight test specimens and one non-flying airframe for static load testing. Ultimately, inflation began to bite and, coupled with the adoption of alternative procurement procedures, this resulted in the number of test-dedicated prototypes being cut to three, although a fourth was restored to the project at a later date.

In broad terms, the resulting B-1 was a variable-geometry aircraft with an overall length of 151ft (46.02m), a wings-spread span of 140.2ft (42.73m) and an overall height to the fin tip of 33.1ft (10.09m), dimensions which did change slightly as a result of "Project Focus". Largely inspired by a desire to reduce cost as far as possible, "Project Focus" rede-

fined performance criteria and weapons load capability, the revamped B-1 which emerged being somewhat heavier but, rather paradoxically, smaller. Now, overall length was 143.5ft (43.74m), height 32.4ft (9.88m) and maximum span 136.7ft (41.66m). Nevertheless, it still relied on a quartet of General Electric F101-GE-100 twin-spool turbofan engines for propulsion, each being rated at a maximum of 30,000lb st (133.4kN) with full afterburner.

The formal Preliminary Design Review was held in July 1971, this being followed in October of the same year by inspection and approval of the full-scale engineering mock-up. Some changes in configuration did occur as a result, generally of a fairly minor nature although they did have some impact on overall dimensions. The existing tail cone was one feature which was revised, as was the degree of sweep of the horizontal tail surfaces. Modification of the ride control vanes on the nose section also occurred, while the double-slotted flap system was eliminated in favour of a single-slotted type. This had the advantage not only of saving weight but also, in conjunction with a minor change in the length of the leading edge slat, providing high-lift characteristics in excess of those laid down in the original requirement.

On completion of this redesign phase, length had risen to 152.2ft (46.39m) and height was now 33.58ft (10.23m). Span remained unaffected, and these were the "vital statistics" of the prototype B-1A (74-158).

If cost considerations exerted some influence on the physical appearance of the B-1, they had a quite

Below: The second example of the Rockwell B-1A to fly was in fact the third aircraft to be built, this joining the flight test programme at Edwards on 1 April 1976. It is shown here on arrival after making the short trip from Palmdale.

dramatic impact on the interior fit. Originally, it had been intended to provide a "custom-made" package of defensive and offensive avionics but this was one of the first areas to suffer, it being decided to employ existing "off-the-shelf" items instead and to pursue a policy of updating during the B-1's service life in much the same way as the B-52 had been improved. In the event, it was also decided to divide the avionics suite into separate defensive and offensive portions and invite industry to tender, the subsequent evaluation culminating in Boeing being chosen in April 1972 to integrate the offensive avionics package. Selection of a contractor to develop defensive avionics took rather longer and it was not until January 1974 that Cutler-Hammer's AIL Division was chosen.

In the meantime, assembly of the first B-1A had begun at Palmdale in 1973. This aircraft was earmarked to investigate flying and handling qualities and it was duly rolled out on 26 October 1974, close to a year after the original target for the maiden flight and almost six months behind the revised date. Programme slippage was an almost inevitable result of cost-consciousness and changing USAF policy with regard to procurement.

A short but highly intensive period of ground testing followed until, on 23 December 1974, the prototype finally left the runway at the start of a 78 minute flight which culminated in a landing at Edwards AFB. Once there, little time was wasted in getting the formal test programme under way, and this was accomplished jointly by personnel from Rockwell and the Air Force Flight Test Center (AFFTC).

With only one prototype expected to be available for well over a year, caution was very much a keynote of the early stage of flight assessment and the first B-1A actually spent very little time aloft during the first six months, flying on average about once a week. However, the amount of data generated during each sortie was considerable and it was processing capability as much as anything else which influenced the pace of development flying. Even though progress was slow, the flight envelope was gradually extended, one particularly notable sortie on 10 April 1975 witnessing not only the first inflight refuelling hook-up but also the first time that Mach unity was exceeded, a maximum speed of Mach 1.5 being attained.

Well hidden

The second B-1A prototype (74-159) was also making a significant contribution at this time, despite being well hidden from public view inside one of Lockheed-California's hangars at Palmdale. Assigned to static testing, it spent much of 1975 in a gigantic rig. This programme was completed in July after which it went back to Rockwell's facility to be prepared for flight.

Shortly after this phase of development, Rockwell's hopes for the B-1 received a tremendous fillip on 15 August when the company was awarded a contract for a fourth aircraft. The intention was that this aircraft would approximate closely to the planned production configuration, and as a result it differed quite significantly from its predecessors. One major change concerned a switch to ejection seats in place

Below: Despite its somewhat ungainly appearance when at rest on the ground, the B-1 looks very different in its natural element, this study of the third B-1A quite clearly revealing that it has extremely graceful lines and proportions.

ROCKWELL B-1B
CUTAWAY DRAWING KEY

1. Radome.
2. Multi-mode phased array radar scanner.
3. Low-observable shrouded scanner tracking mechanism.
4. Radar mounting bulkhead.
5. Radome hinge joint.
6. In-flight refuelling receptacle, open.
7. Nose avionics equipment bays.
8. APQ-164 offensive radar system.
9. Dual pitot heads.
10. Foreplane hydraulic actuator.
11. Structural mode control system (SMCS) ride control foreplane.
12. Foreplane pivot fixing.
13. Front pressure bulkhead.
14. Nose undercarriage wheel bay.
15. Nosewheel doors.
16. Control cable runs.
17. Cockpit floor level.
18. Rudder pedals.
19. Control column, quadruplex automatic flight control system.
20. Instrument panel shroud.
21. Windscreen panels.
22. Detachable nuclear flash screens, all window positions.
23. Co-pilot's ejection seat.
24. Co-pilot's emergency escape hatch.
25. Overhead switch panel.
26. Pilot's emergency escape hatch.
27. Cockpit eyebrow window.
28. Ejection seat launch/mounting rails.
29. Pilot's Weber ACES 'zero-zero' ejection seat.
30. Wing sweep control lever.
31. Cockpit section framing.
32. Toilet.
33. Nose undercarriage drag brace.
34. Twin landing lamps.
35. Taxiing lamp.
36. Shock absorber strut.
37. Twin nosewheels, forward retracting.
38. Torque scissor links.
39. Hydraulic steering control unit.
40. Nosewheel leg door.
41. Retractable boarding ladder.
42. Ventral crew entry hatch, open.
43. Nose undercarriage pivot fixing.
44. Hydraulic retraction jack.
45. Systems Operators' instrument console.
46. Radar hand controller.
47. Crew cabin window panel.
48. Offensive Systems Operators' ejection seat (OSO).
49. Cabin roof escape hatches.
50. Defensive Systems Operators' ejection seat (DSO).
51. Rear pressure bulkhead.
52. External emergency release handle.
53. Underfloor air conditioning ducting.
54. Air system ground connection.
55. External access panels.
56. Avionics equipment racks, port and starboard.
57. Cooling air exhaust duct.
58. Astro navigation antenna.
59. Forward fuselage joint frame.
60. Air system valves and ducting.
61. Dorsal systems and equipment duct.
62. Weapons bay extended range fuel tank.
63. Electrical cable multiplexes.
64. Forward fuselage integral fuel tank.
65. Electronics equipment bay.
66. Ground cooling air connection.
67. Defensive avionics systems transmitting antennas.
68. Weapons bay door hinge mechanism.
69. Forward weapons bay.
70. Weapons bay doors, open.
71. Retractable spoiler.
72. Movable (non-structural) weapons bay bulkhead to suit varying load sizes.
73. Rotary dispenser hydraulic drive motor.
74. Fuel system piping.
75. Communications antennas, port and starboard.
76. Starboard lateral radome.
77. ALQ-161 defensive avionics system equipment.
78. Forward fuselage fuel tanks.
79. Control cable runs.
80. Rotary weapons dispenser.
81. AGM-69 SRAM short-range air-to-surface missiles.
82. Weapons bay door and hinge links.
83. Port defensive avionics system equipment.
84. Fuselage flank fuel tanks.
85. Defensive avionics system transmitting antennas.
86. Port lateral radome.
87. Port navigation light.
88. Wing sweep control screwjack.
89. Wing pivot hinge fitting.
90. Lateral longeron attachment joints.
91. Wing pivot box carry-through.
92. Wing sweep control jack hydraulic motor.
93. Carry-through structure integral fuel tank.
94. Upper longeron/carry-through joints.
95. Starboard wing sweep control hydraulic motor.
96. Wing sweep control screw jack.
97. Starboard navigation light.
98. Wing sweep pivot fixing.
99. Wing root flexible seals.
100. Aperture closing horn fairing.
101. Flap/slat interconnecting drive shaft.
102. Fuel pump.
103. Fuel system piping.
104. Starboard wing integral fuel tanks.
105. Leading edge slat drive shaft.
106. Slat guide rails.
107. Slat screw jacks.
108. Leading edge slat segments (7), open.
109. Wing tip strobe light.
110. Fuel system vent tank.
111. Wing tip fairing.
112. Static dischargers.
113. Fuel jettison.
114. Fixed portion of trailing edge.
115. Starboard spoilers, open.
116. Spoiler hydraulic jacks.
117. Single-slotted Fowler-type flap, down position.
118. Flap screw jacks.
119. Flap guide rails.
120. Wing root housing fairings.
121. Dorsal spine fairing.
122. Wheel bay dorsal fuel tank.
123. Main undercarriage leg strut.
124. Port main undercarriage, stowed position.
125. Wheel bay avionics equipment racks.
126. Fuselage lateral longeron.
127. Wing root housing.
128. Engine bleed air ducting.
129. Ventral retractable air scoop.
130. Fuel cooling heat exchanger.
131. Heat exchanger spill air louvres.
132. Rear rotary weapons dispenser.
133. Control ducting.
134. Tailplane longeron.
135. Wing glove section tail fairing.
136. Starboard wing fully swept position.
137. Starboard engine exhaust nozzles.
138. Longeron joint.
139. Automatic stability and control system equipment (SCAS).
140. Tailplane control linkages.
141. Fin root support structure.
142. Fin/tailplane fairing.
143. Fin spar attachment joint.
144. Tailplane tandem hydraulic control jacks.
145. All-moving tailplane pivot fixing.
146. Fin multi-spar construction.
147. Fin leading edge ribs.
148. Starboard all-moving tailplane.
149. Static dischargers.
150. Fin tip antenna fairing.
151. Defensive avionics system receiving antennas.
152. Rudder honeycomb construction.
153. Rudder powered hinges.
154. Two-segment upper rudder.
155. Rudder automatic stability and control system equipment (SCAS).
156. Tail warning radar equipment.
157. Tailcone radome fairing.
158. Lower rudder segment.
159. Tail radome.
160. Defensive avionics system transmitting antennas.
161. Tailplane trailing edge rib construction.

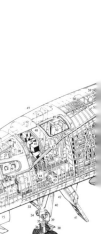

162. Static dischargers.
163. Tailplane tip fairing.
164. Multi-spar tailplane construction.
165. Port all-moving tailplane.
166. Tailplane skin panelling.
167. ALQ-161 defensive avionics system equipment racks.
168. Vortex generators.
169. Ventral communications antennas.
170. Fin attachment fuselage main frames.
171. Rear fuselage integral fuel tank.
172. Tank pressurization nitrogen bottle.
173. Rear fuselage lower longeron.
174. Rear weapons bay bulkhead.
175. Weapons bay doors.
176. Engine nacelle mounting beam.
177. Radar absorbent material (RAM) coating skin panelling.
178. Trailing edge wing root fairing.
179. Aft external cruise missile carriage.
180. Port engine afterburner nozzles.
181. Wing glove section tail fairing.

182. Afterburner ducting.
183. Variable area afterburner nozzle control jacks.
184. General Electric F101-GE-102 afterburning turbofan engines.
185. Engine bleed air tappings.
186. Bleed air pre-cooler.
187. Intake compressor faces.
188. Wing glove articulated sealing plates.
189. Nacelle duct framing.
190. Engine fire suppression bottles.
191. Engine fire suppression bottles.
192. Garrett Auxiliary airborne Power Unit (APU), port and starboard.
193. Airframe mounted engine accessory equipment gearbox.
194. Electrical system generator.
195. Engine fuel system equipment, fully automatic digital engine control.
196. Engine cowling panels.
197. Port single-slotted Fowler-type flaps.
198. Port spoiler panels (4).
199. Spoiler hydraulic jacks.
200. Flap rib construction.
201. Port wing fully swept position.
202. Flap down position.

203. Trailing edge ribs.
204. Fixed portion of trailing edge.
205. Static dischargers.
206. Fuel jettison.
207. Port wing tip fairing.
208. Wing tip strobe light.
209. Fuel vent tank.
210. Port leading edge slat segments.
211. Slat open position.
212. Slat rib construction.
213. Port wing integral fuel tank.
214. Rear spar.
215. Lower wing skin/stringer panel.
216. Wing rib construction.
217. Front spar.
218. Leading edge slat guide rails.
219. Slat screw jacks.
220. Slat drive shaft.
221. Wing skin panelling.
222. Nacelle intake S-duct.
223. Intake anti-radar reflection internal vanes.

224. Boundary layer spill duct.
225. Port engine air intakes.
226. Hinged intake side panel, variable capture area.
227. Four-wheel main undercarriage bogie, inward and aft retracting.
228. Engine intake central divider.
229. External carriage 14 × ALCM maximum.
230. Missile pylons.
231. AGM-86B Air Launched Cruise Missile (ALCM) deployed configuration, maximum of eight missiles internally
232. AGM-69 SRAM air-to-surface missile, 24 internally.
233. B-28 or B-43 free fall nuclear weapons (8).
234. B-61 or B-83 free fall nuclear weapons (24).
235. Mk 84 2000lb (908kg) HE bombs (24).
236. Mk 82 500lb (227kg) HE bombs (84).

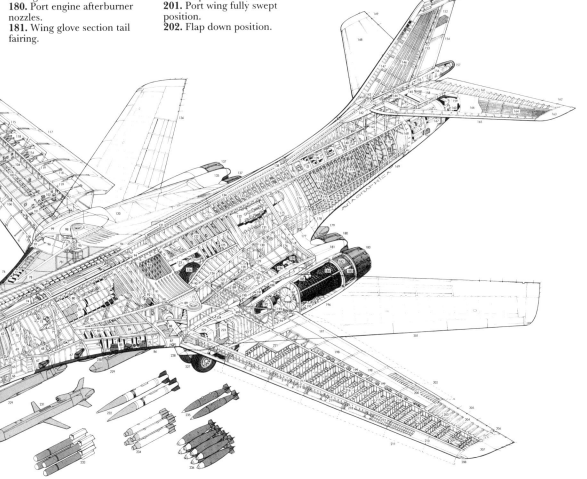

of the crew capsule utilized by the first three B-1s. New engine nacelles were to be a key feature of this fourth aircraft, while it would also incorporate an aft bay for the defensive avionics package.

As it turned out, the third B-1A (74-160) became the second to make its public debut, being rolled out on 16 January 1976. Tasked with evaluating the offensive avionics system, terrain-following flight and weapons delivery, it joined the flight test effort on 1 April 1976 and also proceeded directly to Edwards, as did the second B-1A which made its maiden flight some two-and-a-half months later, on 14 June.

With three aircraft now available, the emphasis of flight testing shifted slightly, the B-1's capability in its planned role being assessed in a series of Initial Operational Test and Evaluation (IOTE) sorties which basically simulated combat-type flying. Successful completion of these in September 1976 cleared the way for the final stage in the process of deciding whether to press on or not. The Defense Systems Acquisition Review Council decided in favour of the procurement of 244 bombers including prototypes on 1 December.

Rockwell and others intimately involved in the project clearly had good cause to be jubilant and their achievements were recognized in April 1977 when the team received the much-vaunted Collier Trophy. Another significant milestone had been passed just a few days earlier with the completion of the 100th test flight. It was against this background that the first of a number of quite cataclysmic shocks was experienced when a Pentagon review recommended a reduction in overall procurement to 150 and, with arms reduction talks under way, President Carter made it quite clear that cancellation was a possibility.

Worse news followed in May. Hard on the heels of the revelation that B-1 unit cost would exceed $100 million, the project began to draw a considerable amount of flak not only from opponents but also from those of a more moderate disposition.

What appeared to be the final blow came on 30

Below: Fourth to fly and first to incorporate the defensive avionics system, B-1A 76-0174 entered the flight stage on 14 February 1979 and, like its three counterparts, began its flying career in a basically white overall colour scheme.

Above: Seen at a later stage in the development programme, the fourth B-1A eventually traded its high-visibility gloss white for low-visibility camouflage and national insignia.

June when President Carter announced that he was no longer in favour of deploying the B-1. Not surprisingly, cost was put forward as a major factor in this decision but it was by no means the only one. Defense Secretary Harold Brown was of the opinion that the air-launched cruise missile represented a far more satisfactory way of achieving an increase in deterrent capability for only relatively modest financial outlay.

Disastrous news

One week later, on 6 July, all B-1 production contracts were terminated by the Department of Defense, and work on the first three production examples ceased forthwith. Naturally, this disastrous news hit Rockwell hard, and the impact was felt thoughout the US aerospace industry, some 8,000 workers being laid off more or less immediately. However, with hardware still flying, Rockwell very quickly came up with a package of proposals for research and development and it was clear that, while virtually everybody else considered the B-1 dead, Rockwell was determined not to let it lie down. Manufacture of the fourth B-1A was permitted to continue, as part of a research and development programme alongside the three existing machines.

Air Force study of the Rockwell propositions culminated in a slimmed-down development programme being submitted to the Secretary of Defense in October 1977, initially under the aegis of the Bomber Penetration Evaluation (BPE) study and, in later stages, as the Near Term Penetrator (NTP), Strategic Weapon Launcher (SWL), Cruise Missile Carrier Aircraft (CMCA), Multi-Role Bomber (MRB) and Long Range Combat Aircraft (LRCA).

Eventually, Congressional approval released funding to permit continued evaluation and the B-1A soon embarked on what transpired to be a three-and-a-half year programme. This period was highlighted by a gradual extension of the performance envelope, B-1A No.2 achieving a maximum speed for the type of Mach 2.2 in early October 1978. Then, on 14 February 1979, the fourth B-1A (76-174) made its maiden flight. It was by far the most sophisticated example of the quartet in terms of equipment fit for it incorporated a full bag of defensive and offensive avionics gear.

By the time the BPE studies terminated on 29 April 1981, the four prototypes had accumulated a grand total of 1,895.2 flight hours in some 347 sorties. Easily the most active aircraft, the third B-1A (offensive avionics testbed) had racked up almost half of the total flight time, with 829.4 hours logged on 138 flights. Second came the original prototype (flying qualities assessment) with 405.3 hours on 79 flights while the fourth, full-capability aircraft had more than compensated for its late start by completing exactly 378 hours in 70 trips aloft. Although B-1A No.2 (structural loads) had the modest total of 282.5 hours and 60 flights, in reality the amount of

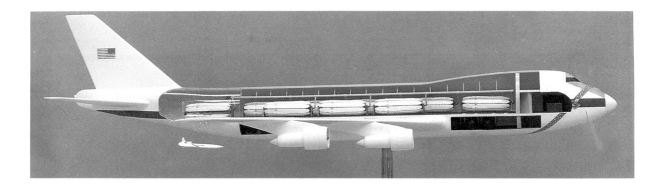

stress it had absorbed almost certainly exceeded that of its counterparts since it had gone "through the wringer" in the Lockheed loading rig at Palmdale.

Even as BPE was proceeding, the first steps in the process of resurrecting the Rockwell bomber were taking place a few thousand miles away in the much quieter environment of the Pentagon in Washington. It was there, on 19 August 1980, that Dr. Zeiberg of the Office of the Secretary of Defense was directed to head a study group to examine bomber alternatives for the future. A broad-based review, it actually consisted of five separate panels, each looking into a different and clearly-defined area. Missions and requirements, threats, aircraft system design, plan and programme and, finally, systems evaluation were the subjects under review, and an interim report was passed to Congress by 7 April 1981.

Four alternatives

Earlier, the USAF's intentions to proceed with development of a new bomber had clearly been signalled on 2 December 1980 when Air Force Vice Chief of Staff General Mathis revealed that it would be known as the Long Range Combat Aircraft (LRCA). Another piece of the jigsaw fell into place on 30 June 1981 when the Air Force Test and Evaluation Center (AFTEC) completed its Manned Bomber Pentrativity Evaluation, basically concluding that there were four logically feasible alternatives. First, the B-52 could be refurbished yet again, gaining much updated electronic equipment in the process; second, the FB-111 could be modified to the so-called "FB-111H" standard which would have offered greater range but would not have been compatible with the ALCM; third, a derivative of the commercial "jumbo jet" could be modified to carry ALCM; and, fourth, the B-1 could be modified for

greater range with increased payload capability, taking advantage of some "stealth" features in the process but losing out in terms of sheer speed.

Futher study of the various options resulted in the B-52 being eliminated by virtue of the fact that its penetration capability would at best be only marginal in the period from 1987 to 1995 when the "stealth" bomber was expected to become available. The FB-111H, on the other hand, seemed to fit the bill quite adequately in those terms but did fall short with regard to payload. The jumbo cruise missile carrier was generally viewed as inadequate in almost every respect save for payload and range, one particularly telling failing relating to its inability to perform conventional-type missions, one of the key recommendations of the AFTEC report.

A modified B-1, however, would be able to satisfy all of these criteria and to all but the most blinkered observer there could only sensibly be one outcome. This was confirmed on 2 October 1981 by President Reagan who announced that SAC was to receive 100 examples of a new version of the Rockwell bomber to be known as the B-1B. Furthermore, it was planned to attain IOC by not later than 1986—a tall order, but one which was by no means insurmountable. Nevertheless, it wouldn't come cheap, initial cost projections anticipating the expenditure of some $20.5 billion in FY1981 dollars but, despite this, Senate approval for funding was forthcoming in December and there now seemed to be little to stand in the way of progress.

To speed the development phase, it was decided to retrieve two of the B-1As from limbo, for there were a number of functions they could perform in the early stages of the 1,100 hour flight test programme.

Accordingly, the second and fourth examples were chosen, the latter being allowed to resume flying in unmodified form in which it attended the Farnborough Air Show in England in September 1982. During this, the B-1A's first and only overseas foray, it clocked up 28 more flying hours, stopping off at Andrews AFB on the outskirts of Washington on its way home to be presented to senior military personnel and politicians. Thereafter, it was grounded for a series of avionics modifications and it did not return to flying status until 30 July 1984, by which time it had acquired an entirely new and much more state-of-the-art avionics suite.

Even as preparations for the Farnborough visit were entering the final stages, work on preparing the second prototype (74-159) had begun, this being quite extensive in that it included fitment of new weapons bay doors, modification of some bulkheads and changes to the flight control system. Initial estimates allowed 21 months for this work but, remarkably, it was completed in just nine months. The modified aircraft flew for the first time in its new guise on 23 March 1983 and embarked on a series of trials which encompassed such diverse aspects as stability and control, flutter and weapons release.

A tragic halt

The good progress then being made was brought to a sudden and tragic halt on 29 August 1984 when 74-159 was destroyed in a crash which resulted in Rockwell's chief test pilot Doug Benefield being killed and the other three crew members sustaining serious injuries. Apparently, the cause of the accident was an out-of-trim condition being allowed to develop during the course of sweeping the wings—once the centre of gravity limit was exceeded there

was nothing that the crew could do to salvage the situation and Major Richard Reynolds wisely elected to utilize the crew escape module. Separation occurred satisfactorily but a malfunction of one of the explosive repositioning bolts resulted in the capsule hitting hard in a nose-down attitude and it was as a result of injuries received in this impact that Doug Benefield died.

The second B-1A had been within four flights of completing its test tasking so although it was a tragic setback, the loss of the prototype had little effect on overall progress. Indeed, the first genuine B-1B (82-001) was just days away from being rolled out at Palmdale, an event which took place on 4 September. Six weeks later, on 18 October 1984, it made a highly successful maiden flight, spending just over three hours aloft in a sortie which involved functional checks of fuel, electrical and hydraulic systems as well as a brief examination of offensive and defensive avionics systems.

Following an engine change arising from foreign object damage, its second flight on 31 October was somewhat shorter but no less successful, and culminated in a landing at Edwards AFB where it joined the Air Force Flight Test Center's B-1B Combined Test Force. One more sortie was made from there in mid-November before the aircraft was grounded for just over two months to permit a number of minor modifications to be made, and it did not return to flight status until late in January 1985. Nevertheless, the early flights boded well for the future and, with more aircraft undergoing assembly at Plant 42, Rockwell had good reason to be well pleased with the way the programme was progressing.

Below: Restored to flight status to aid development of the B-1B, the second B-1A resumed test duty on 23 March 1983 but was destroyed near Edwards on 29 August 1984.

2

The Airframe

ALTHOUGH at first glance more or less identical in outward appearance to the B-1A prototypes, the B-1B is actually very different. This is perhaps best exemplified by the fact that it is considerably heavier, tipping the scales when fully "grossed-out" at no less than 477,000lb (216,365kg), compared to the 395,000lb (179,170kg) maximum take-off weight of the B-1A. Even more remarkable is the fact that virtually all of this massive 82,000lb (37,195kg) weight increase relates to payload: fuel and/or weapons carriage capacity rose quite dramatically at little penalty in terms of basic empty weight.

Naturally, some structural strengthening was required so that the revamped bomber could cope with increased loadings. This was mainly confined to the undercarriage units which were "beefed up" quite significantly, but such changes were mostly compensated for by weight-saving in other areas.

As part of the redesign effort which resulted in the B-1B, it was decided, as far as possible, to take full advantage of recent technological advances which offered every prospect of reducing the B-1B's radar cross section (RCS) or radar "signature" by a quite significant degree. This, in turn, would further limit the chances of detection and, in consequence, enhance its penetration capability and likelihood of survival when operating in hostile airspace. There were a number of ways in which this was achieved. Radar absorbent material (RAM) was used to shroud areas of high reflectivity such as bulkheads situated behind dielectric panels, most notably in the vicinity of the nose and tail radomes plus the wing root fairings which housed much of the defensive avionics gear. The airframe design was also altered to eliminate large flat surfaces and sharp angles which can trap and reflect radar energy. Achieving this resulted in the fore and aft bulkheads being canted slightly so as to act as deflecting, rather than reflecting, surfaces.

Furthermore the engine intakes were radically redesigned to mask the compressor blades which are an excellent reflector of radar signals. In this case, however, modification inevitably impaired performance, air intake geometry being such that high performance can only be achieved at the penalty of high visibility. Fortunately, Mach 2 was no longer a requirement for the B-1B and it was thus possible to adapt the intakes, which involved eliminating the movable ramps, repositioning of the inlet guide vanes, fitment of baffles and the use of RAM.

Application of such "low observable" technology vastly reduced the B-1B's RCS compared to that of the B-1A. It is generally accepted that the B-1B's RCS is only one-tenth that of the B-1A and one-hundredth that of the B-52, which must make it exceedingly difficult to detect, especially when operating in its normal environment at very low level.

Massive undertaking

As prime contractor, Rockwell is responsible for final assembly of the B-1B, a task which is performed in Plant 42 at Palmdale, California, this huge facility actually being owned by the Air Force and used by Rockwell on a kind of leasing arrangement. Not surprisingly, Rockwell makes a substantial contribution to the structure of each B-1B but a considerable amount of work—in the region of 60 per cent—is sub-contracted out and the full list of suppliers involved in this massive undertaking reads like a US aerospace industry directory. No fewer than 3,000 companies are involved in some capacity or other, including, in key areas, Aeronca, Avco, Boeing, Cleveland Pneumatic, Garrett, General Electric, Goodyear, Hamilton Standard, Kaman, Martin Marietta, Singer Kearfott, Sperry, TRW, United Aircraft Products, Vought Aero Products, Weber and Westinghouse Electric.

The B-1B's structure makes extensive use of aluminium alloys and titanium and is hardened to withstand the hazards inherent in a nuclear detonation—blast, heat, overpressure and electromagnetic pulse (EMP) effect. The fuselage is of conventional monocoque-type construction, being fabricated in five main sections, namely forward, forward intermediate, wing carry-through, rear intermediate and rear. The latter two sub-assemblies are produced by the Vought Aero Products Division at Dallas and air-freighted to Palmdale for final assembly. Area rule is a feature of the fuselage design which also embodies a fail-safe stressed-skin structure making extensive use of 2024 and 7075 aluminium alloy.

The use of titanium is principally confined to high load areas or "hot" spots such as the engine bays and firewalls, tail support structure and aft fuselage skinning. The construction also incorporates a five-section boron epoxy dorsal spine extending from the wing carry-through box to the base of the fin, this being one of the few instances of the use of composite materials in the Rockwell bomber. Weapons bay doors are another.

Polymide quartz is used for the nose radome. Other dielectric panels are of glass-reinforced plastic and, as already noted, RAM shrouding is much in evidence in these areas.

The forward fuselage section also contains the crew accommodation area, Hamilton Standard providing pressurization and air conditioning equipment for this. Access is gained by means of a ladder which extends downwards beneath the fuselage just aft of the nosewheel leg. Pilot and co-pilot are teamed up in the usual way on the flight deck, while the defensive systems operator (DSO) and the offensive systems operator (OSO) also work as a team, the DSO being seated to port and the OSO to starboard. The latter occupy a separate compartment just to the rear of the flight deck and linked with it by a small crawl-way. All four crew members may call upon the services of Weber ACES II "zero-zero" ejection seats in the event of having to part company with the aircraft in a hurry. The first three B-1As relied on a crew escape module similar to that of the General Dynamics F-111. Costs and complexity told against this system and the ACES seat was substituted with effect from the fourth B-1A. Supernumerary crew members—one or two instructors and/or check pilots may be carried—are less fortunate, being required to leave the aircraft via the belly hatch in the event of emergency.

Structural mode control system

Another noteworthy feature of the forward fuselage section is the structural mode control system (SMCS) which basically improves ride quality, thus making life generally much more comfortable for crew members when engaged in terrain following or

Below: Seen moments after take-off from Edwards AFB during the early stages of B-1B development flying, the second B-1A eventually donned low-visibility colours similar to those now being applied to production examples of the B-1B.

terrain avoidance flight at low level where turbulence can be near intolerable. Employing small swept-back movable vanes with 30 degrees of anhedral on each side of the nose, in conjunction with the bottom rudder segment, SMCS employs accelerometers to determine turbulence which, if unchecked, could cause movement in lateral and vertical planes. Yawing movement is damped by rudder displacement while motion in pitch is corrected by the nose vanes which have an operating arc of plus or minus 20 degrees. These vanes are made up of graphite epoxy bonded to aluminium honeycomb, with titanium employed for leading and trailing edges.

The B-1B's two weapons bays are located in the fore and aft intermediate sections, the dimensions and capability of these being examined in greater detail elsewhere. The aft intermediate section also houses the main undercarriage, which consists of hydraulically retractable units made by Cleveland Pneumatic and incorporating an anti-skid braking system by Crane Hydro Aire. The tandem pairs of wheels retract inwards and rearwards, lying snugly against the wing carry-through box when in the

stowed position. Moving to the front fuselage again, the twin-wheel steerable nose unit retracts forwards. Goodyear wheels are common to both nose and main members, as are Goodrich tyres.

The variable-geometry wing of the B-1B offers the best of both worlds in that the unswept setting bestows good short-field performance and low-speed handling qualities, while the fully-swept position is employed for flight at high subsonic speed when penetrating at low altitude. Leading edge sweep in the fully forward position is just 15 degrees, rising to 67.3 degrees in fully-swept configuration.

The wing basically consists of three components, the fixed wing carry-through box and two moving outer wing panels. The latter are of conventional two-spar aluminium alloy construction with machined spars and ribs plus one-piece integrally-stiffened top and bottom skin panels.

As with the fuselage, a fail-safe philosophy is

Below: Engine nacelle, trailing-edge flap detail and the location of static discharge wicks are all readily apparent in this close-up view of the second B-1A at Edwards AFB shortly after it resumed development test duty in 1983.

employed in wing construction and the blended wing/body structure bestows additional lift while also providing a convenient place for stowing elements of the defensive avionics package. The outer moving wing panels double as integral fuel tanks, as does the wing carry-through box, which is a massive structure fabricated mainly from diffusion-bonded 6AL-4V titanium.

"Shrink-fitting"

This material is also used for the wing pivot mechanism, a kind of "shrink-fitting" procedure being used for wing attachment with heating blankets being placed on the wing carriage fittings in order to expand them while the pivot pin is immersed in a liquid nitrogen bath which causes it to shrink. With the outer wing panel already in position, all that remains is for the pin to be dropped into place, a procedure which is in fact almost as simple as it sounds, the entire process taking about five minutes and requiring little in the way of protective equipment. Once seated, the pin is unlikely to be disturbed for 30 years.

Sweeping of the wing is accomplished by hydraulically-driven screwjacks and can be achieved by any two of the four hydraulic systems. A torque shaft connecting the two screwjacks inhibits the possibility of asymmetric movement while the sweep actuators are covered by a "knuckle" fairing on the leading-edge, this eliminating the risk of a gap opening as the wing translates aft. Overwing fairings located to the rear of the pivot point blend the wing trailing-edges and engine nacelles.

As far as control surfaces are concerned, the B-1B's wing is fairly generously endowed, incorporating leading-edge slats, trailing-edge flaps and airbrakes/spoilers. With one noteworthy exception, operation is achieved electro-hydraulically by means of rods, pulleys, cables and bellcrank levers. The only variation concerns the two outermost spoiler/airbrake segments on each wing, these being actuated by a fly-by-wire system.

Control surfaces comprise full-span, seven-segment leading-edge slats on each outer panel, drooping 20 degrees for take-off and landing; six-segment, single-slotted, trailing-edge flaps, again on each outer panel, offering a maximum downward deflection of 40 degrees; and four-segment

Above: A truly massive structure, the wing carry-through box—shown here being manoeuvred into position at Palmdale—is made primarily of titanium and doubles as a fuel tank.

airbrakes/spoilers with maximum upward deflection of 70 degrees. Inhibition devices prevent flap and slat operation at wing sweep settings which could cause structural damage, while the outer spoiler sections are automatically locked at speeds in excess of Mach 1. There are no ailerons, lateral control being provided by the spoiler surfaces.

Turning to the empennage, this is a cantilever fail-safe structure featuring a quite marked degree of sweep on all surfaces. Construction is sub-contracted

Below: A set of outer moving wing panels awaits mating at Palmdale. Attachment is accomplished by means of immersing the pivot pin in liquid nitrogen before insertion, cooling in this way causing it to shrink and facilitating fitment.

Above: Festooned with the many umbilical connections which furnish power and other necessary services, the first B-1B (82–0001) had to complete an exhaustive series of pre-flight checks at Palmdale before it was cleared to take to the air.

to Martin Marietta. Materials are a mixture of titanium and aluminium alloy and it is mated to the aft fuselage by means of a double shear attachment, bolts on the tailplane spindle, a vertical shear pin in the tailplane spindle fitting and a shear-bolt joint on the front beam of the torsion box.

Movable surfaces comprise a three-segment rudder of aluminium alloy construction and "all-flying" tailplane. Maximum rudder deflection is 25 degrees to left and right. The tailplane operates collectively for pitch control and differentially for roll control. In the former case, movement may be achieved through an arc extending from 10 degrees up to 25 degrees down, while when operating differentially the arc is plus or minus 20 degrees. As with most other control surfaces, actuation is achieved hydraulically but a back-up fly-by-wire system is available for use in the unlikely event of mechanical failure.

Power for the B-1B is furnished by a quartet of General Electric F101-GE-102 augmented turbofan engines, sited in pairs beneath the fixed centre-section of the wing and, as mentioned earlier, intake geometry was significantly altered to limit RCS following the decision to relax performance criteria. The only moving part now is the outer lip which extends sideways to increase throat area in order to permit the ingestion of more air on take-off.

Rated at 30,000lb st (133.4kN), the F101 embodies modular construction which greatly eases routine maintenance and repair. The provision of numerous borescope ports permits ready inspection of key areas such as the compressor, combustors and turbine blades without the need for time-consuming and costly tear-down. The powerplant is apparently

very reliable in service. One of the few problems known to have been experienced concerned the exhaust nozzle, there being a number of instances of leaves being shed at high speed and altitude during early flight testing. Redesign of the nozzle has, however, succeeded in solving this shortcoming.

Self-start capability

The B-1B also possesses a brace of Garrett auxiliary power units (APUs) which bestow self-start capability when operating away from home base or at a remote austere facility. Indeed, provision of these APUs permits simultaneous engine start, one other useful feature being the installation of an APU starter switch on the nosewheel leg. In a "scramble", the first man to reach the aircraft simply hits this switch and, by the time the crew are at their designated work stations, both APUs will be running and

Above: Power for the Rockwell B-1B is furnished by a battery of four General Electric F101–GE–102 augmented turbofan engines, each of which is capable of generating 30,000lb of thrust. Modular construction eases maintenance and repair.

providing power to aircraft systems, saving seconds which could prove vital in getting the B-1B off the ground.

The B-1B can carry rather more fuel than the original B-1A. Much of the fuselage is set aside for fuel while the movable outer wing panels contain even more, total capacity being in the region of 30,000 US gallons (113,562 litres), sufficient to bestow an unrefuelled range of about 6,500nm (12,045km).

Needless to say, in-flight refuelling capability by either the KC-135A Stratotanker or the KC-10A Extender will increase range further, the B-1B receptacle being situated in the nose section, just a few feet ahead of the windscreen. However, should the

need arise, the weapons bays may also be given over to fuel tanks, while the eight stores stations are compatible with auxiliary tanks which would presumably be jettisoned once their contents had been consumed.

Fuel also plays an important part in aircraft stability. A Simmonds Precision fuel management system is employed to maintain centre of gravity trim automatically as fuel is burned off. Basically, this is achieved by pumping fuel around the various tanks. It is, of course, slightly more complicated than that; fuel weight, weapons load, wing sweep position, Mach number, altitude and attitude all have some bearing on the calculations required.

The B-1B's systems and sub-systems are all either fail-operative or fail-safe. Thus, the loss of any single system will not jeopardize the completion of a mission, while a second failure in the same system will not stop the aircraft from getting home safely. There are no fewer than four independent hydraulic systems, these being responsible for wing sweep actuation, movement of control surfaces, raising and lowering of the undercarriage and actuation of the weapons bay doors.

Similarly, the primary electrical system employs no

Above: The fourth B-1A is prepared for flight from Edwards on an uncharacteristically cloudy day. It was this aircraft which made the B-1A's only overseas visit when it was one of the star attractions at the 1982 Farnborough air show.

fewer than three 115kVA integrated engine-driven constant-speed generators which provide 230/400V three-phase AC power at 400Hz through four main buses. A Sperry-Vickers back-up electrical power system is available for emergencies. The Harris electrical multiplex (EMUX) system, discussed in more detail elsewhere, is basically intended to manage the distribution of electrical power and does this most efficiently at little penalty in terms of both weight and volume.

Another key feature is Sperry's automatic flight control system (AFCS). This quadruplex package actually controls flight path, roll attitude, altitude, airspeed, autothrottle and terrain following. The flight director panel incorporates heading hold, navigation and automatic approach modes. Other elements comprise an AiResearch central air data computer (CADC), a gyro stabilization system, a stability control augmentation system and, as mentioned earlier, the structural mode control system (SMCS).

Above: The flight deck of the first production example of the B-1B reveals that cockpit instrumentation is a mixture of old and new, "needle-type" devices being almost as numerous as the more modern vertical tape displays. Cathode ray tubes dominate both work stations, these being used to display data relating to navigation, terrain clearance, time to target, aircraft attitude, altitude and so on.

Right: The aircraft commander's position looks reasonably uncluttered when compared with older bomber aircraft, one reason for this being the adoption of a fighter-type control column in place of the more traditional and more bulky yoke. Engine throttle controls are conventionally positioned for his left hand while the wing-sweep control can be seen just below the cockpit side coaming.

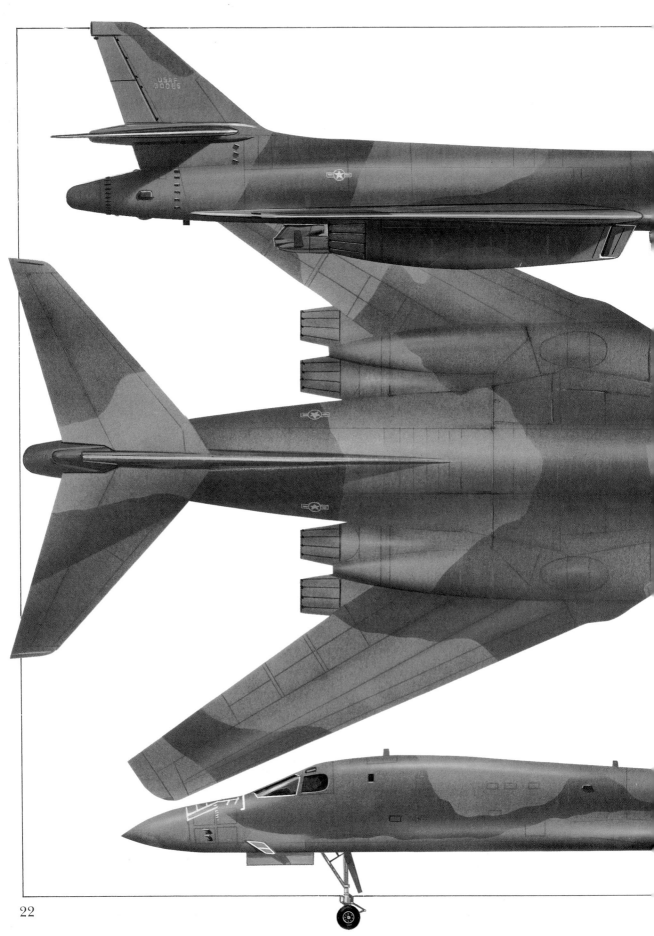

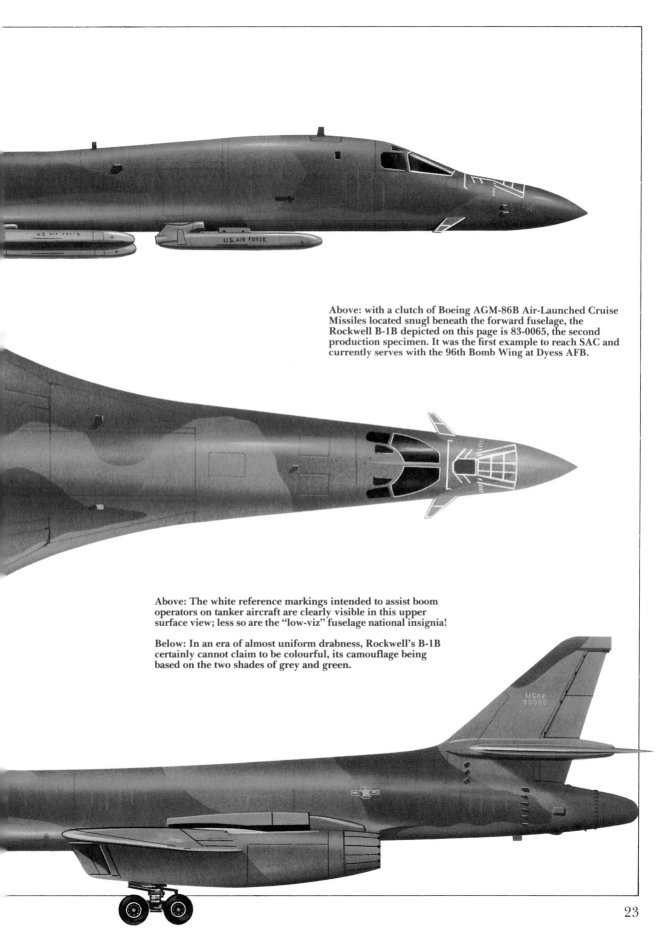

Above: with a clutch of Boeing AGM-86B Air-Launched Cruise Missiles located snugl beneath the forward fuselage, the Rockwell B-1B depicted on this page is 83-0065, the second production specimen. It was the first example to reach SAC and currently serves with the 96th Bomb Wing at Dyess AFB.

Above: The white reference markings intended to assist boom operators on tanker aircraft are clearly visible in this upper surface view; less so are the "low-viz" fuselage national insignia!

Below: In an era of almost uniform drabness, Rockwell's B-1B certainly cannot claim to be colourful, its camouflage being based on the two shades of grey and green.

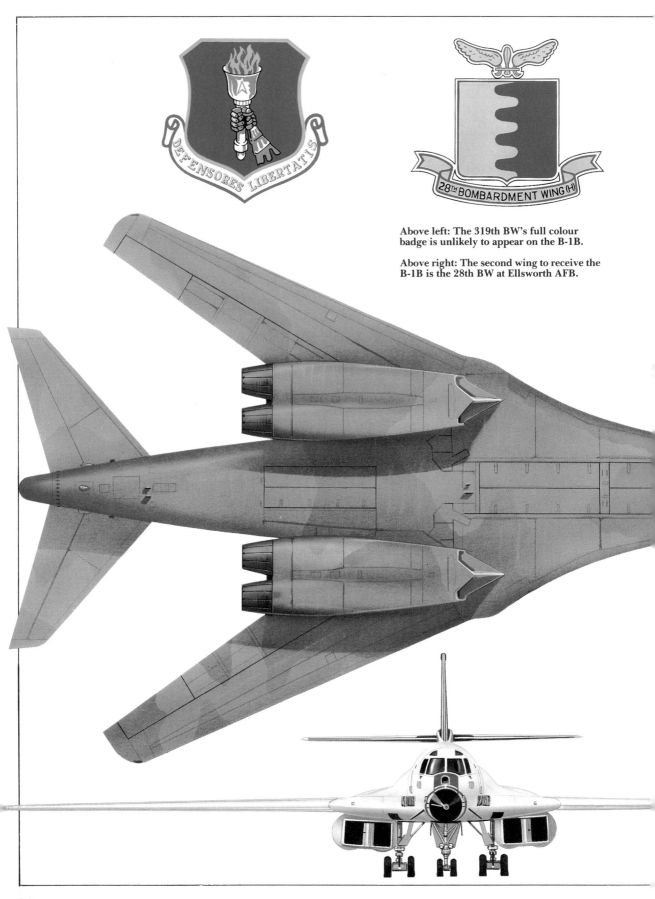

Above left: The 319th BW's full colour badge is unlikely to appear on the B-1B.

Above right: The second wing to receive the B-1B is the 28th BW at Ellsworth AFB.

Right: Black refuelling recepticle reference marks on the nose section indicate that this front view of a B-1B depicts the first production example of Rockwell's bomber.

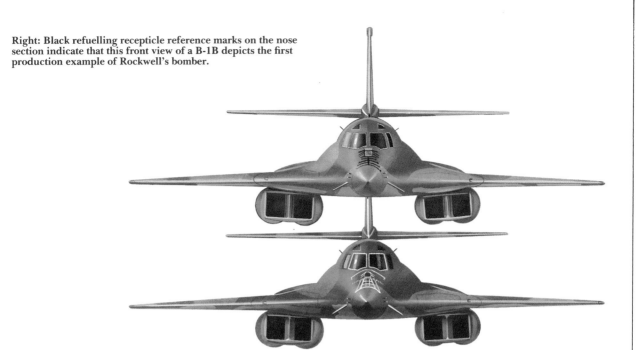

Below: The underside camouflage pattern applied to the B-1B is based upon the use of two shades of grey, although in some conditions it is not easy to differentiate between them.

Above: Representative of the current production-standard Rockwell B-1B, this front view shows the white nose markings that were adopted with effect from the second machine.

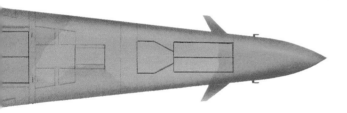

Below (left to right): The three badges depict "low-viz" unit and command markings likely to appear on the B-1B. Those of the 96th BW and SAC (left and centre) are accurate representations while that of the 384th BW (right) is an interpretation based on the full-colour badge.

Left: Following completion of the initial phase of test duty, two of the four Rockwell B-1As were returned to flight status and both made a major contribution in getting the new B-1B programme under way. This front view of a B-1A depicts the second machine soon after it resumed flying.

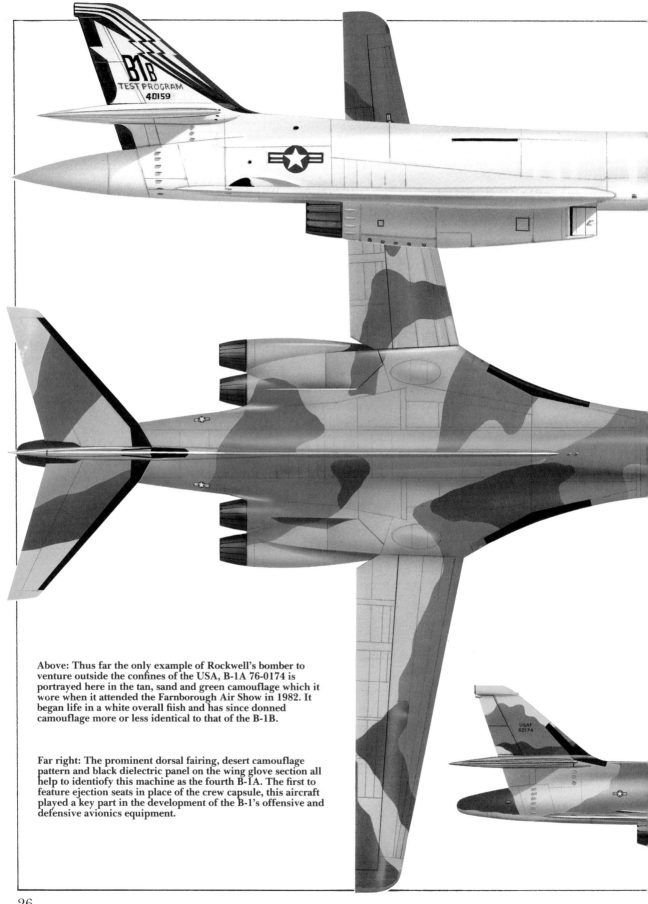

Above: Thus far the only example of Rockwell's bomber to venture outside the confines of the USA, B-1A 76-0174 is portrayed here in the tan, sand and green camouflage which it wore when it attended the Farnborough Air Show in 1982. It began life in a white overall fiish and has since donned camouflage more or less identical to that of the B-1B.

Far right: The prominent dorsal fairing, desert camouflage pattern and black dielectric panel on the wing glove section all help to identiofy this machine as the fourth B-1A. The first to feature ejection seats in place of the crew capsule, this aircraft played a key part in the development of the B-1's offensive and defensive avionics equipment.

Above: Seen with the special blue and red tail markings it wore when it resumed test duty in support of the B-1B project, the second B-1A is the only example of Rockwell's bomber to have been lost to date. It was destroyed when it crashed near Edwards AFB on 29 August 1984, soon after relinquishing its original smart white overall paint job for the rather less attractive but much more realistic low-visibility camouflage.

Below: From behind and with the wings at the maximum sweep angle, the Rockwell B-1B looks decidedly odd, with the widely separated and podded pairs of General Electronic F101 turbofan engines providing a convenient "tunnel" for the external carriage of various items of weaponry. Dark grey and dark green upper surfaces make the B-1B particularly difficult to spot whenever it flies at low level over a temperate landscape such as is found in much of Europe.

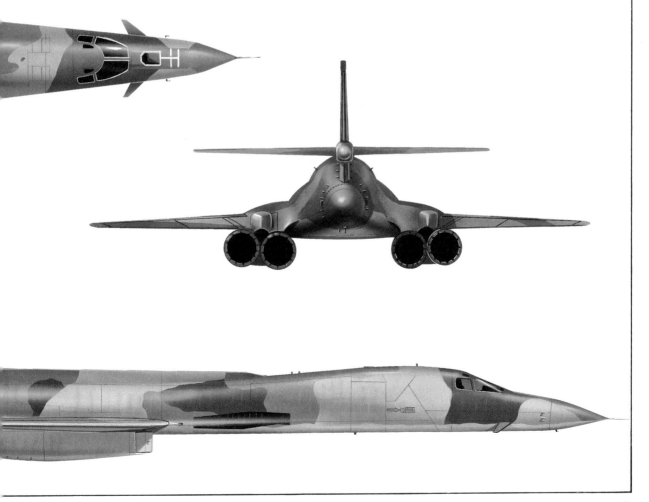

Left: About the only splash of colour which can be found on the B-1B is provided by the reference markings adjacent to the in-flight refuelling receptacle in the extreme nose section. These were originally in black but were changed to white when it was found that boom operators had difficulty in gauging distance accurately.

Below: Should crew members ever have need to part company with the B-1B in a hurry they can call upon the services of the ACES II ejection seat which possesses zero-zero capability and which was first fitted to the fourth example of the B-1A, the previous three aircraft all having a crew escape module rather similar to that of the General Dynamics F-111.

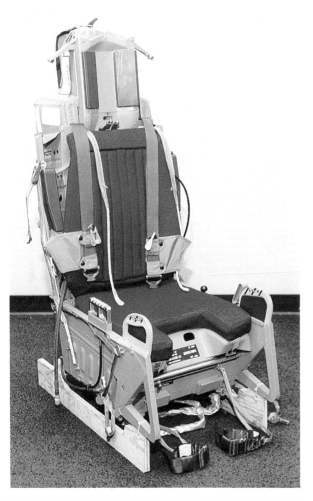

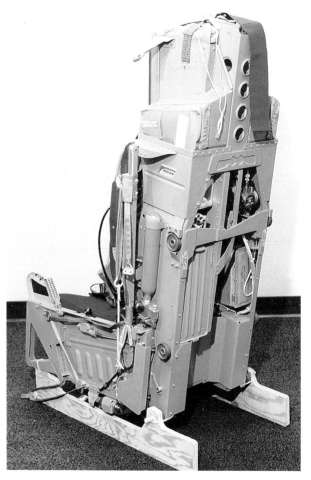

3

Avionics Systems

T HE INCREASING degree of sophistication evident in the design of the modern military aircraft and its associated weaponry has, if anything, been more than matched by a profusion of ever more complex sub-systems intended to "assist" crew members in the execution of their duty. Certainly, the Rockwell B-1B features its fair share of electronic wizardry, being packed with all kinds of avionics "goodies". When faced with such a multiplicity of equipment, it is perhaps all too easy to overlook the fact that the principal mission remains that of delivering bombs. In that respect, the B-1 differs little from the B-17, B-29, B-36 or any of the other types that have gone before; the skill, courage and determination of the crew are by far the most important factors in the success or failure of a mission.

Admittedly, the power of the weapons now being carried has increased tremendously and it is no longer always necessary actually to overfly a target in order to destroy it. Nevertheless, the bomber aircraft still has to proceed to a point where its weapons may be despatched against a specific target or targets, and the avionics systems may therefore be viewed simply as an adjunct to that primary objective.

The B-1B is literally packed with avionics and it is doubtful if it would be able to achieve much without them. The Offensive Avionics System alone comprises no fewer than 66 "black boxes" of 41 different types, the weight of the whole package handsomely exceeding one ton.

Without these avionics the B-1B would be hardpressed to even find its target let alone drop any bombs or launch any missiles. Elements of the avionics suite deal with such diverse aspects as weapons delivery, self-protection and communications. Increasing reliance on avionics generally has meant that succeeding generations of aircraft have been called upon to tote around an ever-increasing amount of kit, often at the cost of payload capability.

However, with enemy defences becoming increasingly deadly, this is felt to be a worthwhile sacrifice, so long as the avionics continue to function satisfactorily.

On the B-1B, a high degree of reliability has already been demonstrated but it is inevitable that elements of the system will at some time or another either fail totally or be capable of only degraded operation. System redundancy goes some way towards eliminating the impact of such failures, but it is obviously desirable for aircraft with non-operable equipment to be returned to "fully up" status as quickly as possible. As a result, the avionics package of the B-1B makes extensive use of line replaceable units (LRUs). Returning an aircraft to full capability is simply a matter of "pulling" the offending "black box" and slotting a serviceable unit in its place. The defective component can then be subjected to bench testing to isolate the cause of failure—once that is known it is usually a relatively simple task to put matters right, the repaired unit then going back "on the shelf" until such time as it is required.

Super-sophisticated kit

Inevitably, in view of the highly sophisticated nature of the B-1B's avionics equipment, computers are extensively employed to process the mass of data that is being continuously generated in flight. Computers are an integral part of the navigation, terrain following, weapons management and delivery, and defensive and offensive avionics sub-systems. IBM's AP-101F is the standard unit on the B-1B.

Having super-sophisticated kit like this is not a great deal of use if the data is unable to reach the correct destination. Rapid data transfer is therefore vital if the crew of the B-1B is to function correctly. Here the data bus and electrical multiplexing (EMUX) systems score heavily, the B-1B actually having four MIL-STD-1553 data buses to receive,

sort, code and then direct information to its destination. Two 2-wire cables are used to control electrical power distribution to sub-systems and avionics gear, engine instruments, environmental control system, landing gear, lights and weapon system operations.

Built-in test capability is also a key element, the Central Integrated Test System (CITS) continually monitoring and verifying the performance of various sub-systems and recording details of failures and battle damage throughout the entire sortie for subsequent post-mission diagnosis and repair. A display panel situated on the bulkhead between the defensive systems operator (DSO) and the offensive systems operator (OSO) work stations enables crew members to be kept fully in the picture with regard to aircraft status.

Apart from certain items of standard government-furnished equipment (GFE), much of which is mainly concerned with communications, B-1B avionics sub-systems fall into two main spheres, offensive and defensive. In both instances, the equipment represents a vast improvement over that originally planned for the B-1A. Boeing was selected as the prime contractor for the Offensive Avionics System (OAS)

Above: Looking much less "busy" than the cockpit, the defensive systems operator's station is nothing if not deceptive, hidden computers displaying data to the DSO by means of multi-function cathode ray tubes, with touch controls.

in April 1972, while the AIL Division of Cutler-Hammer (now the Eaton Corporation) was designated to oversee the Defensive Avionics System (DAS) in January 1974. At that time, of course, it was intended to employ off-the-shelf items as a means of keeping the cost down but the subsequent decision not to proceed with the B-1A proved advantageous in that it enabled both companies to capitalize on advances in this field. Responsibility for flight testing key avionics systems was entrusted to the fourth B-1A (76-0174) which made its maiden flight in mid-February 1979. Eventually, following the decision to proceed with a new version to be known as the B-1B, contracts for production systems were awarded to both companies in June 1982.

Many of the component parts of the OAS are similar to those developed for the B-52, itself the target of a major avionics updating effort in recent times. Boeing's B-1B package is, however, rather more complex and certainly superior, featuring such items as the Singer Kearfott SKN-2440 high accuracy inertial navigation system evolved from that employed by the General Dynamics F-16 Fighting Falcon; Teledyne Ryan's AN/APN-218 Doppler velocity sensor, made up of a single antenna/receiver/transmitter unit; IBM avionics control units (ACUs) similar to those employed by the B-52 for terrain following, plus a mass storage device (MSD) which uses computers to provide programme instructions required for navigation, weapons delivery, bomb damage assessment, defensive system computation and central integrated test functions; a Sperry Flight Systems offensive display package, again essentially similar to that installed in the Stratofortress, incorporating two multi-function visual display units (VDUs) located at the OSO's work area and a third for the DSO, plus an electronics display unit and a video recorder; Sanders Associates electronic cathode ray tube (CRT) display units based on those originally intended to go in the B-1A, to enable the DSO first to analyse developing "threats" and then initiate whatever countermeasures he deems to be appropriate; and, finally (and also a spin-off from the B-52), Sundstrand data transfer units to record mission and flight-related data for subsequent study.

Perhaps the most important single element of the OAS equipment, though, is the Westinghouse AN/APQ-164 multi-mode offensive radar system.

Evolved from the F-16's AN/APG-66 unit, it emerged the winner in a straight fight with a Hughes offering combining features of the F-15 Eagle's AN/APG-63 and the F-18 Hornet's AN/APG-65 radars. Incorporating technological advances designed to reduce the risk of detection, the AN/APQ-164 is a dual-channel multi-mode coherent pulse Doppler radar utilizing a fixed low-observable phased-array antenna with scanning being accomplished electronically. Since the antenna is canted downwards, the chances of detection are reduced, for enemy radar emissions will almost certainly be deflected in a downward direction rather than reflected straight back to the source. Use of radar absorbent materials (RAM) on the bulkhead, which serves as a mounting point, further reduces the risk of detection.

Those associated with the programme are naturally reluctant to say too much about the AN/APQ-164 radar but it is generally accepted that it may operate in any one of no fewer than 13 modes, ranging from real beam and high resolution ground mapping through terrain following and avoidance, to ground moving target indication and ground moving target

Below: The offensive systems operator's station and the adjacent Central Integrated Test System console which reports on the status of key elements of the B-1B. Access to the flight deck is gained via a tunnel beneath the CITS.

tracking. In-flight refuelling rendezvous, weather detection and avoidance, ground or air beacon, monopulse measurement and high altitude calibration are the remaining modes, but these are perhaps of less significance in view of the B-1B's primary role.

Since the aircraft will be expected to penetrate at low level, it follows that ground mapping and terrain following are likely to be the most valuable modes. In real beam mapping, low pulse repetition frequency (PRF) is employed in conjunction with non-coherent pulse-to-pulse frequency hopping to provide a small-scale radar map of the terrain ahead of the aircraft. Computer-adjustment results in vertical map presentation and it is known that Doppler beam-sharpening may be used to enhance definition.

Synthetic aperture radar

High resolution ground mapping utilizes synthetic aperture radar (SAR) techniques to provide a picture which apparently approximates closely to that achieved with low-grade photography and which is said to be sufficiently good to "allow a landing on a damaged airfield at night or in bad weather, with recourse to ground-based landing aids".

The system is employed in en route navigation, for updating positional information by means of pre-programmed waypoints and in the terminal target location and attack phases of a mission. Data generated by the radar is presented on a radar display or, in certain circumstances, on one of the multi-function CRTs at the OSO's station.

Updating of navigational information by use of a pre-programmed waypoint is accomplished quite simply. The display places cross-hairs over the calculated position. Deviation will then be readily apparent, appearing as a displacement when compared with the real point which will show up on the screen. All the operator then has to do is move the cross-hairs to the correct location, and this automatically updates navigation and puts the aircraft back on the desired track.

Terrain-following capability is rather more variable since the quality of ride and the altitude may be determined by the crew, who can specify hard, medium or soft ride. Any one of 11 clearance altitudes can be selected, the lowest of these reportedly being just 200ft (60m). In TFR mode, radar emissions are intermittent, the scan pattern being

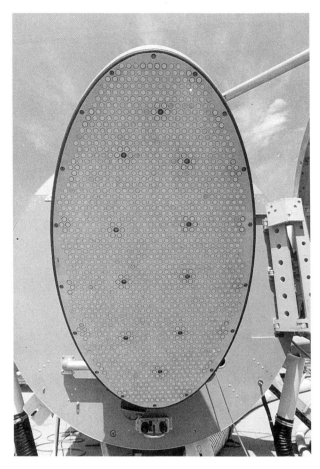

Above: A vital component of the B-1B, Westinghouse's APQ-164 phased-array radar antenna was first tested in flight on a BAC 1-11. Ground mapping and terrain following are just two of the many modes of operation that are possible.

programmed to "look ahead" at intervals which are dependent on the type of terrain being overflown. Thus, for instance, over a flat landscape it will scan less frequently than when operating over undulating terrain. Scanning range is about 10nm (18.5km). Data passes to radar and navigation computers which determine the flight profile, and this is then passed to the terrain-following control unit which automatically commands the flight control system to take whatever avoiding action is necessary.

In terrain-avoidance mode, however, it is the prerogative of the crew to initiate avoiding action. Once again, any one of 11 altitudes may be specified, the radar scan then providing visual reference to obstacles which exceed the preset height on both the pilot's and co-pilot's CRTs. It is then a relatively simple matter either to fly around them or climb to pass over them.

When the OAS package was being put together by Boeing, serious consideration was given to including a Hughes forward-looking infra-red (FLIR) sensor and a Dalmo-Victor low light level television (LLLTV) set. These would have combined to form an electro-optical viewing system with similar capability to that possessed by the B-52G/H. In the event, this requirement seems to have been allowed to lapse but there is a possibility that the Low Altitude Navigation and Targeting Infra-Red at Night (LANTIRN) system may one day be adopted, unlike another piece of equipment which one might have expected to find its way into the B-1B. This is a satellite signal receiver for the Navstar Global Positioning System, but it appears that there are no plans to incorporate this.

If the principal function of the OAS equipment can be defined simply as that of enabling the B-1B to find and attack its target, the DAS can equally basically be described as the means with which it protects itself as it progresses through hostile enemy airspace. In truth, of course, it isn't quite as simple as that but there is no doubt that, in its own way, the B-1B's suite of defensive equipment is no less "smart" than the OAS.

Based on the ALQ-161 system which was originally conceived for the B-1A, the DAS also benefited from the hiatus in development of the parent bomber and, in its current form, it is expected to permit the B-1B to penetrate existing and projected defensive networks until well into the 1990s when the aircraft may be supplanted by Northrop's ATB. Even so, a fair amount of "growth" potential is built-in and there seems to be no reason why the Rockwell bomber should not take advantage of on-going research aimed at countering new "threats" as and when they appear.

As installed on the B-1B, control of the AN/ALQ-161 system is exercised by a group of easily reprogrammable digital computers. The various elements of the package are "wired-in" to a dedicated data bus network which will allow for incorporation of any on-going upgrades considered necessary to adapt to future threats until well into the 21st Century.

Varied threat

The very nature of the radar threat is, of course, extremely varied, encompassing ground-based air defence control networks associated with anti-aircraft artillery and missile systems to airborne equipment carried by fighter interceptors and early warning and control platforms. Between them,

Below: The trailing edge lift-augmenting devices which provide such good low-speed handling qualities are clearly visible in this view of the second B-1A (74–0159) during the course of B-1B development test flight work from Edwards AFB. The definitive low-visibility colour scheme adopted for this aircraft shortly before its crash provided a dramatic contrast to the far more visible finish previously applied.

this multiplicity of systems will offer an extremely dense hazardous environment which, if not effectively jammed, could well result in the destruction of a B-1B intent on penetrating to a target.

It is the AN/ALQ-161's task to disrupt this array of equipment, a function which is accomplished in large part by numerous Northrop (Defense Systems Division) jamming transmitters working in conjunction with Raytheon phased-array antennae. In practice, AN/ALQ-161 is a fully automatic system. Control of jamming signals is handled by several digital computers, although the DSO may choose to override these if he feels that circumstances dictate human intervention. For the most part, though, the DSO's main function is perceived as being a supervisory one.

Left to its own devices, the computer network has the ability to control the jamming chains so rapidly and efficiently that each is able to deal with many "threat" radars at the same time. The large number of jamming chains are mainly located in the B-1B's aft fuselage adjacent to the vertical tail and in both port and starboard wing root fairings, so as to provide full 360-degree coverage.

Another key element of the AN/ALQ-161 system and one that might fairly be called the B-1B's "ears" is the complex network of receiving antennae, receivers and processors. These are wholly integrated with the emitters, a novel feature of the AN/ALQ-161 at the time of its debut but one which greatly accelerates response time. Indeed, so fast does the system work that new hostile signals may be detected, classified and jammed in just a fraction of a second. In addition, integration in this way enables the receiving system to detect new signals and continue to monitor old signals, all the while jamming in the same frequency band.

This is achieved by continuous monitoring of jamming transmitter output and adjustment of the receivers.

Naturally, the DSO will be anxious to know precisely what is going on at any given time and to this end his work station incorporates three display units as well as numerous controls so that he may "interfere" if he so desires. Communication with the AN/ALQ-161 package is handled by a dedicated data bus which also provides system status reports to the CITS. One other useful facility is a kind of self-test system known as Status Evaluation and Test (SEAT) which enables the system automatically to divert electronic signals around failed or degraded elements. In this way full jamming capability can be maintained against signals considered to present the highest degree of "threat".

Like the OAS suite, the defensive avionics package is no lightweight, the present AN/ALQ-161 system tipping the scales at around 5,200lb (2,360kg), and that does not take into account cables, displays and control units. It also places great demand on the B-1B's electrical supply, consuming about 120kW of power when working flat out.

Other non-avionics related defensive equipment includes chaff and infra-red flares, housed in a dispenser in the fuselage top aft of the crew compartment. Use of these may be accomplished either automatically, by the AN/ALQ-161 system or manually, by the DSO, who is also responsible for keeping a careful check on remaining stocks.

Below: The B-1B's defensive avionics suite is nothing if not impressive, being made up of no fewer than 107 individual units. These are distributed at strategic points around the airframe so as to provide 360 degree coverage of "threats". Automation permits near-instantaneous response by measures ranging from jamming to the ejection of chaff and/or flares.

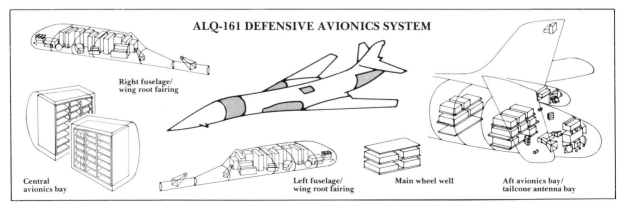

ALQ-161 DEFENSIVE AVIONICS SYSTEM

Right fuselage/wing root fairing

Central avionics bay

Left fuselage/wing root fairing

Main wheel well

Aft avionics bay/tailcone antenna bay

4
B-1B Weaponry

ALTHOUGH perceived as being primarily an element of the strategic nuclear deterrent triad, the Rockwell B-1B is in fact rather more flexible than that, for it does possess the ability to operate with conventional weaponry. However, until the so-called Advanced Technology Bomber (ATB) becomes available in the mid-1990s, the B-1B will understandably be more concerned with deterrence than with conventional warfare applications. In consequence, nuclear weaponry is obviously of far greater significance at the present time.

Two of the three weapons bays are located adjacent to the wing glove area and these can, in effect, be transformed into a single 31ft 3in (9.53m) bay by the removal of the non-structural intervening bulkhead. The third weapons bay—measuring 15ft (4.57m) long—is situated in the aft fuselage, between the engines. Although most Emergency War Order (EWO) missions probably anticipate use of the interior space for weapons, it is just conceivable that all three weapons bays could be set aside for the carriage of additional fuel, with the offensive payload then being mounted externally on any or all of the eight stores stations situated beneath the fuselage.

When compared with the older B-52, the B-1B's internal capacity is truly impressive. For instance, while the Stratofortress can carry at most just four gravity bombs in its weapons bay, the B-1B may take as many as 24, obviously depending on the weight and size of the device concerned.

Four basic types of gravity weapon have been mentioned in connection with the B-1B—the B28, B43, B61 and B83. The B-1B may carry a maximum of 12 B28 or B43 bombs internally but, in view of the fact that these are now in the process of being phased-out of the nuclear arsenal, it seems unlikely that they will be employed in an operational capacity. However, the newer B61 and B83 bombs are expected to figure prominently, with the latter having been identified as the "major gravity weapon for the B-1". No fewer than 24 of each can be housed internally, the B61 being a "lightweight" bomb in terms of weight, falling into the 750–850lb (340–385kg) class. At least six B61 variants are known to exist and there are reported to be four yield options in the 100–500 kiloton range. SAC-assigned weapons are probably confined to the upper bracket.

In distinct contrast, the B83 is a far heavier weapon, weighing in the region of 2,400lb (1,090kg) and coming into the megaton class in terms of yield. Development was initiated in FY1980, with produc-

Below: Responsibility for early phases of B-1B weapons test work fell to the second B-1A, depicted here just moments after ejecting a dummy AGM-69A Short-Range Attack Missile from the forward weapons bay. SRAM is, in fact, just one of a variety of nuclear weapons which may be carried by the Rockwell B-1B, others being ALCM and gravity bombs.

tion getting under way during 1983 and Initial Operational Capability apparently being achieved in 1984. Intended to replace the older B28 and B43 bombs, the B83 is parachute-retarded, can be delivered at any altitude from 150ft to 50,000ft (46-15,240m) and may be set for air or ground detonation.

The B-1B may also operate with either the Boeing AGM-69A Short Range Attack Missile (SRAM) or the Boeing AGM-86B Air Launched Cruise Missile (ALCM). As is the case with the B-52, a rotary launcher is used for internal carriage of SRAM, the B-1B being able to accommodate a maximum of three launchers, each with eight missiles for a total of 24. Able to deliver a 170–200kT warhead at high speed (Mach 2.8 to 3.2) over a maximum range of about 137 miles (221km), SRAM is expected to give way to the Advanced Strategic Air Launched Missile (ASALM) from 1990 onwards but in the intervening period will form an important element of the B-1B's armoury.

As far as ALCM is concerned, the dimensions of the launcher confine internal carriage to just the forward bays, it being necessary to reposition the bulkhead to accommodate it. Once again, the number of weapons carried on the launcher is eight and in this configuration the B-1B will probably benefit from the provision of an additional fuel tank ahead of the ALCM equipment plus another larger tank in the aft bay.

Cruise missile carrier

Since ALCM was one of the principal factors in the decision to cancel plans to deploy the B-1A, it is particularly ironic to note that the B-1B is now viewed as a cruise missile carrier. Indeed, this mode of operation will probably assume even greater importance in the mid-1990s when the ATB begins to reach SAC units. The B-1B would then probably switch from penetration to stand-off methods of employment.

ALCM itself is a rather more sedate delivery system than SRAM in that it possesses a maximum speed of about 435kt (805km/h). What it lacks in

Left (top to bottom): A sequence of pictures portraying an Edwards-based B-1B delivering a parachute-retarded inert nuclear device, the weapon concerned probably being a B83 which is earmarked for carriage by the Rockwell bomber.

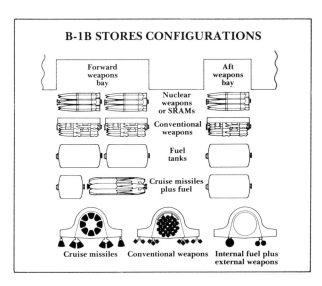

B-1B STORES CONFIGURATIONS

Forward weapons bay		Aft weapons bay	
		Nuclear weapons or SRAMs	
		Conventional weapons	
		Fuel tanks	
		Cruise missiles plus fuel	

Cruise missiles   Conventional weapons   Internal fuel plus external weapons

Above: As this drawing indicates, versatility is the keynote of the B-1B weapons bays, various loads of ordnance and/or fuel being possible. In addition, further weaponry, such as cruise missiles or bombs, may be carried externally.

Below: Like the earlier B-52, Boeing's AGM-69A SRAM does feature in B-1B armament options, the use of a rotary launch device permitting internal carriage of some 24 SRAMs.

speed, though, it more than compensates for in range and "stealth", being able to deliver a 200 kiloton warhead with great accuracy over a distance of about 1,300nm (2,500km) at very low level, which makes it exceedingly difficult even to detect, let alone destroy. ALCM has been the subject of some improvement since it began to enter service with SAC's B-52G-equipped 416th BW in the summer of 1982. Current production is of the AGM-86C model which is slightly faster than the AGM-86B and also possesses about 10 per cent greater range.

All eight external stores stations may be used for the carriage of weapons. In the penetration mode, however, this capability is unlikely to be widely used, largely because hanging bombs or missiles on the B-1B would seriously compromise the "stealth" features by making it far more "visible" to enemy radars. As far as bombs are concerned, though, external carriage of the B28 is limited to eight, unlike the B43, B61 and B83, 14 of which may be carried.

Both SRAM and ALCM are also cleared for external loading, the B-1B being able to accommo-

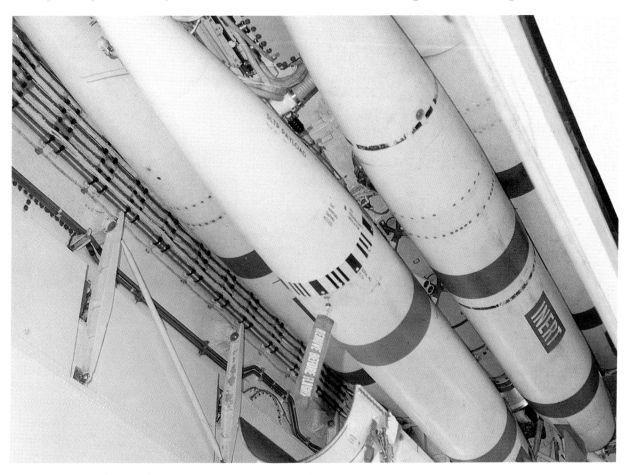

date 14 examples of either kind of missile in this fashion. ALCM would appear to be the weapon best suited for carriage in this way for it does lend itself to the much in-vogue "shoot and penetrate" philosophy in which missiles are sent on their way from a position of relative security well outside enemy terri-tory. Having disposed of ALCM, the B-1B could then proceed to deliver internally-housed SRAM and/or gravity weapons in the usual way, taking advantage of its stealth characteristics and avionics equipment to penetrate at low level.

Conventional ordnance

Turning to conventional ordnance, the B-1B is compatible with a variety of weapons presently to be found in the US arsenal. "Iron" bombs naturally feature strongly and, indeed, the type's capability in this area is quite fearsome. The aircraft can tote as many as 128 Mk.82 500lb (227kg) bombs, 84 being housed in the three weapons bays with the rest carried externally. Alternatively, for a heavier "punch", 24 Mk.84 2,000lb (908kg) bombs may be accommodated internally, with a further 14 on racks beneath the fuselage. Alternatively, 14 CBU-75 munitions dispensers may be carried externally, pre-

Above: Weapons separation and delivery trials actually began during the B-1A era, the third aircraft being shown here soon after dropping an inert SRAM from the forward weapons bay. Other trials were conducted with conventional ordnance. In the course of time, the newer ALCM will also be accommodated internally, on an eight-round launcher in the forward bay.

sumably employed in conjunction with internally-housed bombs.

In maritime surveillance and patrol, a role which it could theoretically be called upon to perform at some future date, the B-1B will be able to utilize Mk.36 and Mk.60 mines, and can reportedly carry a maximum of 26 examples of the latter. In addition, provision for the rather more sophisticated McDonnell Doug-las AGM-84A Harpoon air-to-surface anti-shipping missile apparently also exists with only minimal mod-ification to software and stores stations being re-quired.

Finally, although the B-1B is expected to rely primarily on its internal avionics to confuse enemy radar networks as to its precise whereabouts during the penetration phase of a mission, there is always the possibility that a modicum of active defensive capability will one day be provided. This is most likely to take the form of a short-range infra-red homing missile of which the AIM-9L Sidewinder is perhaps the best known contemporary example.

5

The B-1B in Service

THE B-1B's service career is still in its infancy, but quite a bit of detail has emerged with regard to planned operational deployment and force disposition. SAC's current proposals are based on the acquisition of just 100 examples of the new bomber. However, in the light of recent Rockwell-originating proposals for continued production, it is by no means inconceivable that SAC will eventually obtain more aircraft, the manufacturer having suggested that an additional 50 B-1Bs should be procured as a follow-on batch utilizing FY87 funding. In late 1986 no official response had been forthcoming but it seems likely that this idea is being given serious consideration.

The distinction of introducing the B-1B to operational service has been entrusted to the 96th Bomb Wing at Dyess AFB, Abilene, Texas, and most of the first 30 aircraft to roll from the Palmdale production line have been delivered there. Previously equipped with the B-52H, the 96th BW's 337th Bomb Squadron was the first combat-rated element to receive the B-1B and it was expected to attain initial operational capability (IOC) by September 1986 when it should have built-up to its full strength of 15 aircraft.

In fact, the situation at Dyess is perhaps slightly more complicated than it might at first appear, for the 96th BW also acts as a parent to the B-1B crew training unit. Known in service parlance as the 4018th Combat Crew Training Squadron (CCTS), this was formally activated on 15 March 1985 and

Below: The scene at Offutt AFB, Nebraska, on 27 July 1985 when Secretary of the Air Force Verne Orr handed the first operational example of the B-1B over to SAC's commander, General Bennie L. Davis, in a fairly modest ceremony.

will, when at full strength, have a total of 11 Primary Aircraft Authorized (PAA) examples of the B-1B plus three back-ups. Thus, there will eventually be a total of 29 B-1Bs at this Texas base.

One other unit at Dyess which does deserve brief mention is Detachment One of the 4201st Test and Evaluation Squadron which is intimately involved in the process of bringing the B-1B "up to speed". Although mainly concerned with follow-on test and evaluation functions, Det.1 was also tasked with training an initial cadre of instructors for the 4018th CCTS, but it is interesting to report that it actually has no aircraft of its own.

Future squadrons

Moving a few hundred miles northwards, Ellsworth AFB in South Dakota is the second B-1B base, having received its first aircraft in January 1987. Due to complete the process of re-equipment about eight months later, assuming that there is no change in disposition, Ellsworth will eventually be home to a total of 35 B-1Bs, three of which are considered as back-ups. Parent unit will be the 28th Bomb Wing which will exercise control over two fully-fledged Bomb Squadrons. One of these seems

Above: Pictured during the course of its third trip aloft, B-1B 20001 flew for the first time on 18 October and soon moved to Edwards AFB where, like the B-1As before it, it was immersed in a heavy test schedule.

certain to be the 77th BS while the other may well be the 37th BS.

Both of the other two bases which will support B-1B-equipped Bomb Wings will have a total of 17 examples of the new bomber assigned, one aircraft at each base serving as a back-up. At Grand Forks AFB, North Dakota, the 319th BW will dispose of the B-52G in favour of the B-1B, with delivery of the latter set to begin in about August 1987. Identity of the operating squadron is not known but it seems reasonable to assume that it will be the 46th BS which has utilized the Stratofortress continuously since the 319th BW was activated in February 1963.

At McConnell AFB, Kansas, however, the identity of the B-1B squadron is by no means so easy to predict, for the 384th Air Refueling Wing has been out of the bomber "business" since way back in 1964 when it disposed of the B-47E Stratojet. At that time known as the 384th BW, it was resurrected as an Air Refueling Wing in December 1972 and has controlled two KC-135 Stratotanker squadrons since the autumn of 1973. More recently, it became the first

SAC unit to re-equip with the much-improved CFM56-engined KC-135R and it will be redesignated as a Bomb Wing in time for delivery of the first B-1B, an event scheduled to occur in January 1988. The author's guess is that the forthcoming B-1B squadron will be the 544th BS.

Hand-over of the 100th and last B-1B is due to take place on 30 April 1988 and will signal the close of the deployment phase although it will, naturally, be some months before the 319th and 384th BWs achieve IOC.

Testing accomplished with the B-1A from Edwards AFB in the early 1980s did much to smooth the way for the B-1B and relatively little time elapsed between the first flight and handover of a production specimen to SAC. Formal roll-out out of the initial B-1B—there was no prototype in the generally accepted sense—took place at Palmdale on 4 September 1984. The aircraft (82-001) made its maiden flight just six weeks later when, on 18 October, it left Palmdale for Edwards. Once there, it soon joined the 4200th Test and Evaluation Squadron, a unit traditionally associated with development of any new aircraft or air-launched weapon system earmarked for service with SAC. The first of two aircraft destined to serve with the 4200th TES on a long-term basis—the second will be B-1B No. 9 (84-049)—it was soon heavily committed to a variety of test projects.

In the meantime, preparations at Dyess forged ahead. This long-time SAC base had been identified by President Reagan as the first B-1B operating location on 21 January 1983. At that time the 96th BW had barely completed conversion from the B-52D to the B-52H but the latter model was to be operated only briefly and the unit began disposing of the Stratofortress in August 1984. By January 1985, all the "Buffs" had gone, leaving just the KC-135As of the 917th ARS in residence.

Formal ceremonies

The first aircraft to join SAC was technically 83-0065, this being the subject of formal ceremonies conducted at the Offutt AFB headquarters near Omaha, Nebraska, on 27 June 1985. General Bennie L. Davis, SAC's Commander-in-Chief, "received the keys" from Secretary of the Air Force Verne Orr who had accompanied the 4200th TES flight crew which ferried the B-1B north from Edwards. It had originally been intended that this B-1B would proceed to Dyess two days later but it unfortunately sustained engine damage on arrival at Offutt when bolts retaining the flapper door assemblies on the port side came adrift.

Below: Changes in markings were introduced with effect from the second production example of the B-1B (83-0065) which had white refuelling reference marks on the nose section.

Although replacement engines were soon despatched to Offutt, these were also damaged during a ground test, leaving those responsible with little option but to change the programme schedule. As a consequence, General Davis and the B-1B crew members flew initially to Edwards where they picked up B-1B No.1 (82-001) and it was this aircraft which, decorated with a 96th BW badge and the name "Star of Abilene", was the first to arrive at Dyess. In the event, its stay there was brief, the real "Star of Abilene" (83-0065) materializing at Dyess on 8 July, following yet another engine change.

By the end of September 1985, the number of B-1Bs on USAF charge had risen to five, most of these going to the 4018th CCTS which was hard at work checking out future instructors on the type in anticipation of assuming full responsibility for combat crew training. In fact, although training of aircrew is certainly the most visible aspect of the work performed by a CCTS, the unit's brief is rather more

Above: With the wing set in the fully forward position, the second B-1A cruises serenely over California. The most obvious difference between this and the production B-1B is the tail cone, that on the latter aircraft being more rounded.

Right: The high-visibility nose markings stand out starkly against the drab camouflage on this B-1B as it formates for a photographic session, rather unusually with the wings positioned at maximum sweep angle for high-speed flight.

wide-ranging than that, for it is no good having superbly qualified pilots, navigators and electronic warfare officers if there is nobody to undertake the often-overlooked but nevertheless vital maintenance and ground support tasks. As a result, the 4018th is also engaged in providing tuition to those whose job it is to perform these functions.

At the time of writing, the 96th BW is in the final stages of receiving its full authorized complement of 29 aircraft, the last example being due to arrive at Dyess in November 1986. Thereafter, attention will switch to the Ellsworth-based 28th Bomb Wing.

43

6

Colours and Markings

ALTHOUGH numerous colour schemes and markings options were studied, only three basic finishes have been worn by the Rockwell bomber in the course of its 12-year flying career, and it is the most recent of these that is now being applied to fully operational aircraft. In broad terms, these finishes relate to three distinct chapters in the aircraft's history, namely B-1A, the development phase leading up to the B-1B and the B-1B itself.

All four B-1A prototype aircraft (40158-40160 and 60174) began life in a basically gloss white overall finish, with large-size national insignia on both sides of the aft fuselage section, above the port wing and below the starboard wing. "U.S. Air Force" legends were displayed in deep blue on each side of the forward fuselage just aft of the cockpit. Blue "USAF" inscriptions were carried above the starboard wing

and below the port wing. Five-digit serial numbers in the form indicated earlier were present on both sides of the vertical tail surfaces, in black, while the usual profusion of warning notices could be seen in the vicinity of the cockpit.

In addition, the first three aircraft are known to have carried a single digit number on the nosewheel door in black, this relating to the order in which they were built. Thus, B-1A 40158 was number "1" while 40160 was number "3". B-1A number four (60174) may also have been marked in this way. A further small splash of colour was provided by the red turbine warning lines around the aft portion of the

Below: Photographic reference markings on the engine nacelle were perhaps the most distinctive feature of the third B-1A, shown here taking fuel from a SAC KC-135A. The basic colour was white, with black dielectric panels providing some relief.

engine nacelles, while black dielectric panels were also much in evidence at various points on the fin, fuselage and nose section.

All four B-1As also displayed Strategic Air Command's insignia on both sides of the nose section, although the positioning of this seems to have varied slightly. On the first three aircraft, it seems to have originated from a point roughly mid-way between the cockpit and the tip of the radome, the blue and white star-spangled sash sloping aft in the usual fashion and being surmounted by a full-colour SAC badge. On the fourth B-1A, however, this insignia had been moved slightly aft and now originated more or less adjacent to the front of the cockpit.

Unique features were few. Nevertheless, both of the first two aircraft carried prominent red and white "barber's pole" pitot tubes extending forward from the nose radome. The third and fourth B-1As were decorated with highly visible black photo-reference markings on the outer surfaces of the engine nacelles, the latter machine also featuring a large black dielectric panel in the vicinity of the wing glove roots, presumably associated with the defensive avionics suite. These colours appear to have been retained for the duration of the B-1A test effort which terminated in April 1981.

The restoration of two B-1As (aircraft 2 and 4) to airworthy condition for test duties in conjunction with the B-1B project resulted in a number of noteworthy changes. First to resume flying activity in this role, 40159 initially appeared in very much the same scheme it had previously worn, the most visible evidence of its new role being furnished by red and blue trim on the fin which also bore the legend "B1B Test Program", the designation appearing in blue while the rest of this inscription was in red. This scheme seems to have been retained until shortly before 40159 was destroyed, it apparently still being thus adorned in July 1984 when engaged in SRAM ejection trials at one of the ranges near Edwards. By August, however, it had donned the definitive low-visibility paint.

B-1A number four was, in fact, the first of the breed to adopt camouflage battledress, being restored briefly to flying duty in the late summer of 1982 to appear in the static display at the Farnborough Air Show. In this instance, though, the colours used were visually much more appealing,

Below: The red and white "barber's pole" nose probe and the colourful fin trim help to identify this aircraft as the second B-1A, seen here over the Pacific Ocean soon after returning to flight status in support of the B-1B programme.

shades of tan, brown and green being applied on the upper surfaces and fuselage sides in what was basically a disruptive pattern. Undersides were matt white and full-colour national insignia were applied in the usual four positions although much reduced in size. The only other distinguishing markings were "USAF 60174" inscriptions in black on the vertical tail.

B-1A 40160 is reported to have adopted a basically similar scheme, being noted at Edwards in "desert camouflage" during the summer of 1985, but quite why this was done remains a mystery. In the intervening period, 60174 had also been repainted in the new low-visibility colours and it was probably finished thus when it returned to flying duties at the end of July 1984.

"European One"

In the meantime, it appears that consideration was given to adopting a basically grey overall camouflage finish, light grey being used in the vicinity of heat-sensitive areas such as the flight deck and electronics bay and dark grey elsewhere. Ultimately, this was not proceeded with, the USAF choosing to employ a variation of the "European One" camouflage instead.

This is the definitive camouflage and it is applied to all production B-1Bs. The precise hues employed are very hard to define accurately for they seem to vary remarkably according to differing lighting conditions. However, it appears that there are three basic shades, comprising green (FS 34086), dark grey (FS 36081) and light grey (FS 36118). The scheme is applied overall, about the only relief being provided by low-visibility national insignia in the usual locations and by USAF titles and serial numbers on the fin in black. In addition, the first aircraft to be delivered to Dyess also carried the name "Star of Abilene" and a 96th BW badge on the forward fuselage but these markings were almost certainly unrepresentative. Insignia of this nature are likely to be limited to a low-visibility unit badge on the starboard side of the nose with, possibly, a SAC badge to port.

About the only other distinguishing feature that is worth mentioning relates to the markings applied to assist boom operators in aerial refuelling hook-ups. These were initially black and were soon found to be unsatisfactory in poor lighting conditions or at night, as "boomers" experienced great difficulty with regard to depth perception. To make life easier, it was decided to use white for these markings and this has vastly improved matters.

Above: Beyond the fact that it is quite obviously a B-1B, this study of an early production example of one of Rockwell's bombers flying just above the cloud tops is not too revealing. Indeed, the demarcation lines between the various shades of the low-visibility and allegedly radar-absorbent camouflage paint are virtually indistinguishable.

Below: When viewed against the European environment, the green and grey based B-1B camouflage pattern is probably extremely effective, rendering it hard to spot at low level. Over California, however, the story is very different, this example of the B-1B standing out like the proverbial sore thumb as it flies low over typical desert terrain.

Above: Featuring the definitive operational camouflage paint job complete with high-visibility nose markings, the second B-1B gets airborne from Rockwell's facility at Palmdale. The subject of the formal handover ceremony at Offutt in July 1985, 30065 was eventually given the name *Star of Abilene* soon after joining the 96th Bomb Wing at Dyess AFB, Texas.

APPENDIX I: ROCKWELL B-1B SPECIFICATION DATA

Powerplant
Four General Electric F101-GE-102 augmented turbofan engines, each rated at 17,000lb st (75.6kN) dry and 30,000lb st (133.4kN) in afterburner.

Dimensions

Wing span (fully spread):	136ft 8.5in (41.67m)
(fully swept):	78ft 2.5in (23.84m)
Length overall:	147ft 0in (44.81m)
Height overall:	34ft 0in (10.36m)
Tailplane span:	44ft 10in (13.67m)
Wing area (gross):	1,950sq ft (181.2sq m) approx

Weights and Loading

Empty, equipped:	192,000lb (87,090kg)
Internal weapons load:	75,000lb (34,019kg)
External weapons load:	59,000lb (26,762kg)
Maximum fuel load:	195,000lb (88,450kg)
Typical conventional weapon load:	64,000lb (29,030kg)
Maximum take-off weight:	477,000lb (216,365kg)
Maximum wing loading:	244.6lb/sq ft (1,194kg/sq m) approx

Performance

Maximum level speed:	Mach 1.25 approx
Low-level penetration speed at approx 200ft (61m):	exceeds 521kt (600mph, 965km/h)
Maximum unrefuelled range:	approx 6,475nm (7,455 miles, 12,000km)
Service ceiling:	49,000ft (14,934m)

APPENDIX II: PRODUCTION DETAILS

B-1A Model

Build Numbers	Serial Numbers
1-3	74-0158/0160
4	76-0174

B-1B Model

Lot	Build Numbers	Serial Numbers
I	1	82-0001
II	2-8	83-0065/0071
III	9-19	84-0049/0058
IV	20-54	85-0059/0092
V	55-100	86-0093/0140

 PRINTED IN BELGIUM BY INTERNATIONAL BOOK PRODUCTION